MW01175044

IS YOUR LIFE A M.E.S.S?

DEBUNKING THE MYTHS OF A.D.H.D. ONE STORY AT A TIME

BY

Christina Johnson-Quan, B.PAS, B.Ed., M.Ed.

M.E.S.S MANAGEMENT, EDUCATION, STRATEGIES AND SUCCESS

I was ruminating one day about the mess my life was in. The mess my finances were; then the mess my truck was, and the mess in my office. I kept asking myself, where was my motivation? But, all my life I've had motivation to do things, especially when I'm instantly praised for my performance. So I figured there has to be something positive in all this MESS. I needed to start to make some changes and in order for me to make some changes, I needed motivation. So, I created an acronym. I started to manage the ADHD characteristics; I educated myself about my ADHD, and then created strategies. I realized, even with all this MESS, I could be a SUCCESS.

~Christina Johnson-Quan

IS YOUR ADHD LIFE A MESS? DEBUNKING THE MYTHS OF ADHD ONE STORY AT A TIME

© 2013 Christina Johnson-Quan

ISBN: **978-1499378740**

Cover photography is done By Allison Squire with Modern Storyz Photography

www.modernstoryzphotography.com

Publisher: Christina Johnson-Quan, Saskatoon, SK

WHY READ ABOUT A MESS?

Most people have a general idea about ADHD. But over time, what I'm always hearing from teachers, educators, parents, and children is, "I never knew that." So, if you're the person with ADHD and you often wonder why you seem different, and never really had answers to your questions? If you're always watching your spouse do something catastrophic and think how can he/she do it again, and again? If you know someone with a diagnosis or even suspect ADHD, then this book is for you!

This book will educate you and entertain you. It might even encourage you to change your views of ADHD. There's a stigma to having any diagnosis, and that's a different story altogether. This book will touch on the rippling effect of undiagnosed ADHD, as well as the many challenges and barriers people encounter. It will enlighten you about the co-existing behaviors of ADHD and it will use evidence based research to debunk some of the myths people have about Attention, Deficit, Hyperactivity Disorder.

The examples in this book are my real life stories. These are just small snippets of what the life of a person with ADHD can be like. I work as an educator, and an ADHD consultant. I also coach people to overcome their academic challenges, and learn the barriers to their success. I can only hope that over time people begin to accept ADHD as a neurobiological impairment of the frontal cortex of the brain. In fact, I challenge children every day to learn about what makes them tick. So maybe after you read about my MESS you might just understand what makes you tick.

ABOUT THE AUTHOR

Christina Johnson-Quan works at the Learning Disabilities Association of Saskatchewan where she engages in a number of opportunities to advocate for people with disabilities and ADHD. She grew up in Prince Albert, Saskatchewan; continued her post-secondary pursuits at University of Saskatchewan and University of Regina. She works as an ADHD Coach; an academic strategist, and an educator. She facilitates and delivers workshops on a variety of informative; educational topics about Attention Deficit Hyperactivity Disorder, and Learning Disabilities.

Christina has been an advocate for people with disabilities for a number of years. She has been employed with The Learning Disabilities

Association of Saskatchewan since 2006, where she began as a tutor. She struggled academically all through her undergrad and later was successful in achieving her Master's in Education from the University of Saskatchewan. In 2010, she was diagnosed with ADHD, anxiety, and a Learning Disability. Now as an ADHD coach, she promotes academic interventions for students with ADHD; she bridges the gap between home and school by educating and advocating for her clients. She has evolved and morphed over the years as an educator and has finally found her passion; it is **educating others and debunking the myths of ADHD, one story at a time.**

A life spent making mistakes is not only

more honorable, but more useful than a

life spent doing nothing.

~ George Bernard Shaw

MY ADHD WORLD AS I KNOW IT

It was an interesting start to a new career as I sat in the airplane and stared out the window at the Prairie fire and the land of the living skies. As I disembarked and awaited the awkward greeting from my parents and family, I was in a daze of confusion combined with excitement, torment and anticipation. For years I had disappointed my family, begged for money to settle my financial woes, broken their hearts and shattered their dreams. I can still remember the look on their faces as I boarded a plane in 1997 with nothing but a backpack on my back and $200.00 in my wallet. I was heading West chasing a dream of love and freedom. I continued to live with unpredictable boundaries, with a passion for discovery and a goal to eventually find what it was I was looking for. In the Spring of 1997, as a graduate from the Education Program from the University of Regina, I was a first-year teacher; I was fresh and ready for almost anything, but I knew nothing. However, I had figured out three things for sure: I was good with kids, I was a great athlete, and I was always on the go. I thought about why I kept changing jobs; why I was so impulsive; why I couldn't focus or pay attention at home, school or work. I knew that I was different, and I knew there was something wrong.

In 2010, I was diagnosed with ADHD. To be given a professional diagnosis suggests the characteristics must interfere with daily life; they must be prolonged, and they must cross over into different environments. Following a variety of unmanageable events and experiences, I discovered there are a number of different ways to manage ADHD. It starts with education about the diagnosis and then developing coping strategies. The process involves a combination of people, because it's not just about trying to help the person with ADHD there's more to it. It becomes more about the other people in their life that also need education, support and strategies. So in retrospect there has to be a team approach to managing and helping the ADHD brain. Management is a multi-modal approach. Multi modal means: a variety of supports through education for teachers, parents, and families; using medication as an intervention, and having strategies in place.

As I reflected on my first **seven** jobs as a teacher, I realized the administration wanted me to accomplish their goals, but I had other things in mind. Let's face it, I was easily distracted, forgetful, disorganized and my lessons would always ripple into educational moments where I was suddenly off topic. I had students who wanted to learn how to study; I had students who were interested in figuring out how to save for a car; and I had students wanting to know how to manage work, school, and a newborn at home. But my administrators had expectations. They expected me to teach Shakespeare, literature and sometimes even Math. These were subjects that I had never really put much effort into. I was a physical education teacher, with a special education minor. I was often teaching English or Foods and Nutrition. Now, many years later, I work as an ADHD Coach. I recognize the impact ADHD has on other people. When I accepted the challenge of working as an ADHD Coach I realized I had a different perspective on coaching because after all, it takes one to know one. During my coaching sessions, I have this illusion, about my personal experiences; my adventures, my troubles and travels, it could actually encourage others. Maybe they could even develop coping strategies before they hit rock bottom. What I realized is the supports, the creative interventions, and the coping strategies were great for the ADHD brain. But, what I didn't know was teachers and parents had limited knowledge about ADHD; they don't know how to advocate for interventions and strategies. It was apparent to me that there was a lack of education for parents and teachers about understanding the impact of ADHD on children. In response, I decided to share with other people the snippets of experiences that have affected me over the years, and how these moments are common for children as they attempt to understand their own ADHD. I am determined to express the value in learning about ADHD, and learning a variety of coping strategies in order to feel successful. I hope that people reading MESS will learn what it's like to be ADHD; how valuable it is to learn how to advocate for others, and learn about ADHD. The information in the following pages presents personal experiences. Using a narrative approach I will give you insight from an ADHD perspective. You will learn the impact of relationships with family members and parents. The relationships with teachers and professionals; how it affects the eventual outcome and achievement of children with ADHD.

"EDUCATE YOURSELF."   "It's one of the best strategies I've ever used. I educate myself about what's getting in the way of me succeeding and then I make it my vocation to learn how to manage it and use creative interventions."

~Christina Johnson-Quan

UNDERSTANDING YOUR CHILD AND YOUR CHILD UNDERSTANDING HIM OR HERSELF

People understand me so poorly that they don't even understand my complaint about them not understanding me.

~Soren Kierkegaard

For people like me with ADHD, when everything around me is coming at me at different speeds and intensities, it can be overwhelming. Suddenly I realize that things are really messed up! I've had a history of trying to deal with the issues of ADHD that repeatedly interfere with my success. It never seems to get any better and clearly never goes away. My need for reflection on what I've done, and why I've done it again and again, happens daily. My reflections evolve from a question: is it anxiety; can it be my organizational issues, or is it procrastination? Then all the other characteristics I have to deal with as well. But, somewhere in my mixed up filing cabinet that some call a brain, I know I've got to figure out what the problem is and then solve it. At any rate, here's the stage I'm at in my life: I'm aging painfully, growing intellectually, maturing finally, and I can sometimes remember that I'm 41, but I'm managing. My short term memory is often next to nothing, and my long term memory is somewhat distorted. However, some of the broken roads and northern stars have lead me on a path of self-discovery, and by the way, also led me astray.

I had swum through some oceans; hiked through some valleys, then thumbed my way through the rockiest of mountains, to reach deserts so I could ride on the backs of camels, and at last but not least swam with elephants all before I knew I was ADHD. The diagnosis of ADHD is different for everyone. For me, it encourages spontaneity, lowers my inhibitions, and leads me to follow my instincts and impulsivities. Most people with ADHD struggle in many areas: organization, time management, procrastination, follow-through, planning, financial disasters, low self-esteem and much more.

As you read through my MESS you'll begin to recognize that we all have behaviors very similar to

ADHD. But, the difference is, for those that just can't manage and seem to mess up in every environment; then the realization that many of their problems exist because they have ADHD. In order to be diagnosed, the ADHD characteristics must interfere with success. So, if you have no problems with successes and the characteristics don't interfere in your daily life, then you don't have ADHD.

"The gamut of characteristics can have a significant impact on nearly every aspect of a person's life. It's fair to say that everyone has the characteristics of ADHD. But, people with a diagnosis will satisfy diagnostic criteria, suggesting the characteristics will have been apparent since early childhood, the characteristics will be impacting their life in a negative way, and the characteristics appear in more than one environment."

~Christina Johnson-Quan

COMMON ADHD

CHARACTERISTICS

The Main <u>Thing</u> is to <u>Keep</u>

The Main Thing The Main Thing.

~ *Stephen Covey*

Earlier research made the assumptions that there were three subtypes: over activity, inattentiveness and poor inhibitions. However, Russell Barkley (2007) identified a combination of additional characteristics that affect people with ADHD. In order for people to manage ADHD, they need to understand what characteristics affect them and how. Furthermore, Barkley suggests ADHD often has a number of co-morbidities that interfere with success. Co-morbidities are several other problems or characteristics that exist at the same time as the diagnosis of ADHD. Many will encounter issues with being able to advocate for themselves, explain their diagnosis to others, and interact socially. It reminds me of situations where I never quite got it. I'd sit with this strange look on my face staring into space; I'd lean in for someone to clarify, but never recognize how loud I was talking or even how close I was. I was socially awkward in some instances because of a number of the ADHD characteristics.

> **Strategy:** Start with identifying the characteristic; then stop and think, in order to problem solve. The result is gratifying because you will learn how to manage the situation.

There's a variety of ways that people can collect information to determine the characteristics. I found several web sites where there were lists and lists of characteristics. I research ADHD; I learn about the characteristics, I teach myself creative interventions and I focus on change. As a means of educating myself I collected the characteristics all together into one document. It's a well-used hand out now. Not only for me but for the children I coach and the parents I consult with.

In the following pages you'll understand how it's a combination of delays and lags in the way the brain is working. Medical research indicates the neurotransmitters aren't firing the way the brain needs them to fire. I often share a visual experience that helps others understand what's going on in the ADHD brain. Imagine the ADHD brains were like fireworks. My brain sends that firework straight up into the sky but there's no fabulous light show. Neuroscience suggests there needs to be some kind of neurotransmitter that makes the light show happen. When the light show happens, the brain is ready to perform key tasks such as: planning, organizing, focusing, filtering, managing anxiety, follow-through, impulsivities, etc., etc. The result, the brain is attempting to use the neurotransmitters such as: serotonin, dopamine and norepinephrine; the usage is efficient and effective. But, if the light show isn't spectacular that means there's a problem in how the brain makes, and uses those neurotransmitters. The neurotransmitters carry messages that will enable the brain to function for the situation. You might recall the old "fight or flight" scenario. This suggests the brain is firing the neurotransmitters in order to accomplish tasks and goals. Without the neurotransmitters working and doing their job effectively, the gamut of ADHD characteristics often interfere with everyday success.

We've all been here before. **TIRED, SPACY AND IRRITABLE.** I often explore with parents some simple little myths and one is: Children don't purposely set out to ruin your day, and most of all they don't plan to be tired, spacy and irritable. Children don't intentionally set out every day to be a disruption. Neurotransmitters in the brain are released in order to reduce the effects of being tired, spacy and irritable. Each neurotransmitter will affect the brain differently. The affected neurotransmitters of the ADHD brain are usually serotonin, dopamine, and epinephrine/norepinephrine. Note: Epinephrine and norepinephrine are neurotransmitters, as well as hormones. AKA (adrenalin and noradrenalin). Another myth: Give a child Ritalin. The truth is every child with ADHD will experience different characteristics (you'll see some of these on Page 27) based on how their brain is utilization and replacing key neurotransmitters.

On the following page is a little cheat sheet to separate what the neurotransmitters do, as well as further understand the importance of having neurotransmitters firing correctly. The information comes from Kids on Meds, a reference for determining the role of medications in the treatment of different disorders of the brain.

SEROTONIN:

- Affects sleep patterns and aggression
- Used for depression
- Helps with **IRRITABILITY**

DOPAMINE:

- Focus
- Attention
- Concentration
- Reinforces behavior
- Helps with being **SPACY**

NOREPINEPHRINE:

- Brain adrenalin for alertness
- Fight/flight
- Helps with being **TIRED**

The following pages will help to summarize the broader swath of impairments that affect individuals in their education, social life, family life, and home life. Not everyone displays the same characteristics, and bear in mind some trigger other co-existing behaviours as well.

DISTRACTIBILITY

Many people with ADHD are easily distracted. I've found myself in farmer's fields not realizing how I got there; in parking lots confused about why I was there, and in meetings where I've missed the whole meeting. I've also been in lectures where I can't even recall who the professor was. Being easily distractible characterizes ADHD more than anything else. This affects a person's ability to maintain attention to tasks and be productive.

Strategy: Allow energy to be channeled into another area by using kinesthetic hands on activities. Such as: creative note taking strategies, fidget tools, rubber bands, and small tactile tools.

The result is often effective because it allows the brain an opportunity to process, recall, and organize thoughts, by reducing interference and distractions.

Strategy: Little respectful nudges can keep some people focused; setting up an effective environment to reduce distractions and teaching students how to direct their focus in order to reduce distractions.

People have ideas and inspirations for all kinds of projects that never quite get completed. I know, because I have a closet full of half started but never finished albums, memory books, crafts and sewing projects. Luckily I have a husband that picks up the loose ends for me, without him things are really a MESS.

INATTENIVENSS AND HYPERFOCUSING

Two other challenging characteristics are inattentiveness and hyper focusing. On the flip side, these can also be seen as strengths. Specialists suggest a person will completely forget about their surroundings when they're doing something they enjoy. Ideally I can focus so intensively I can go into a trance-like state. In these short bursts of hyper focusing, I'm not distractible, and I can actually get work done. My parent's on the other hand would have suggested the trance like states I was in were rather irritating and annoying for them.

> **Strategy:** Talk to them, not at them from another room. They won't process it. They're super focused; you will have to go to them and gently nudge them to direct their attention to you.

My parents had difficulty getting my attention or shifting my attention without a pretty serious meltdown. When I was hyper focused I was easily startled, easily angered, and then the result was often-- impulsive range. Many people with ADHD can use hyperfocus to their advantage. I remember times in university when it was crunch time; I didn't really manage along the way, but when I knew I had to, I was able to get things done; pull it off and do okay. It didn't stop there. In my early days of teaching I'd leave the preparation, marking, and planning all to the end. At that point my stress levels were so high that my brain would send out another nice neurotransmitter called cortisol. Then it was a sudden, instant ability to focus; I was able to get tasks accomplished and manage to follow-through on my objectives. When people have a diagnosis of ADHD the Dr's, and professionals involved in the diagnosis indicate characteristics are pervasive, permanent, and cause problems. To translate that means: If I had problems with focus and attention at home, this could affect my follow-through with assignments and projects at school. So in retrospect, my follow-through will also be affected by attention and focus at work, and in social environments. The distractibility and focus issues will never go away, and likely create some negative consequences. But with education, strategies and possibly a medical intervention there may be less negative consequences. Many specialists, researchers, and psychotherapists have determined the characteristics cross over from environment to environment, and in order to manage success, and failures, we need education. Let's get back to hyper focus, this characteristic can also be seen as a motivator. I know when I find something I'm interested in, I become very productive. I wanted to train for a marathon a while back, so for four months I trained. I focused every day on training. When I ran in the race; I couldn't help but notice the beautiful sunny morning, as the streets of Vancouver were littered with people. I finished in 95th place, out of 1257 competitors! I was focused, I had a goal, and my reward was gratifying. According to a number of key researchers, authors and specialists, hyper focusing can be the difference between success and failure (Robin, 1998).

FORGETFULNESS

Forgetfulness is another characteristic that can have an enormous impact on people with ADHD. It can be present to the point where it has a tremendous impairment on the child academically and in the home. I often hear parents and teachers say comments like, "He should be able to do it by now, all the rest of the children his age can." "I want him to learn to do it on his own." "She shouldn't need me to do it for her, and besides she should be more independent by now."

Strategy: I like to suggest using empathy and give help where help is needed. He is forgetful; she will need your help, so help him to help himself, and give her what she needs to be successful.

In order to help people that forget, it starts with being able to advocate for them as well as empathise with them. Forgetfulness is one of those executive functions of the brain; if it's out of sight, it's out of mind. A key to unlocking a mystery of the ADHD brain is to accept that the ADHD brain is lagging in the working memory. So when they say, "I forgot." They really did forget.

> **Strategy:** Remind them; help them to remember but don't ridicule them, and make them feel stupid. It doesn't help to judge them or direct negative attention to them. Just help them to remember.

About five years ago I was staying with my brother, and I was doing some multi-tasking. I was doing some dishes, cleaning the laundry room, and scrubbing the bathroom. I was running the water in the bathroom to wash the floors when the phone rang. So I went into the kitchen and answered the phone. After that I continued on doing something else, went upstairs, got dressed, and left the house to run some errands. Upon returning, I came in through the laundry room door and there was a flood of water coming into the garage. I had forgotten the water was running and never did get back to the bathroom to finish cleaning the floors. This is just one simple event in my life that could have been a catastrophe. But I'll have to leave that story for another book.

Strategy: Develop increased self-awareness skills. I've discovered that some stories are on a need to know basis and sometimes there's a difference between interesting and relevant.

To carry on with forgetfulness, this leads into another key area - being messy and disorganized. Some things just seem so overwhelming that it's hard to even know where the beginning is and where the end might be.

Strategy: Giving the ADHD person direct instruction will reduce confusion; reduce miss understanding and feelings of being overwhelmed. Tell them **what** to do.

I remember times as a child, my mom would send me to my room to clean; cleaning was never really a success. I never knew where to start, or even how to start or what to do. I believe most children with ADHD need direct instruction. I know for myself, tell me where to start, and I will start there. Tell me what to do, and I can do it. But, if you leave me with gray areas I get nothing accomplished. I use a particular philosophy with my students. I tell them to look at things like a puzzle. We all start somewhere and it's different for everyone. But there is a start, and there is a finish. Then with parent's I tell them, "direct instruction." "Tell them **what** to do."

DISORGANIZATION, CONFUSED AND JUMBLED THINKING

Disorganization, confused and jumbled thinking these are other characteristics that plague many ADHD children and adults. Individuals with ADHD will often live their lives in a whirlwind, with everything around them in a disorganized chaos.

> **Strategy:** Use technology as a friend; introducing APPS, computer generated calendars, and organizers.

Professionals suggest tools like computers and electronic organizers encourage structure and organization (Kutscher, 2007). ADHD is a combination of lags; if disorganization is left unattended, it can lead to confused and jumbled thinking. This is a common characteristic because so much is happening so fast. It just seems there is no time to think. Many of us with ADHD really cannot stay on one trail of thought. I feel like I have ten TV stations on all at once, and don't know which one to focus on. This is simply the body's reaction to, too much stimuli.

> **Strategy:** Change the environment and you'll change the behavior.

I know in restaurants I need to have my back to the crowd or I never process what my husband is saying. Change the environment and you'll change the behaviour. My thoughts can bounce around in my mind like a balloon in the wind tied to a string. It's very difficult to have peace of mind. Some people are so affected by this that they cannot carry on a conversation without bouncing from one topic to another, and they tend to ramble on without any rhyme or reason (Robin, 1998). I know that when my husband asks me questions about my plans and projects I really have a difficult time externalizing those plans. I become so confused and jumbled.

Strategy: Give time for processing. Ask one question and wait for a response. Then probe for more information, but don't continue asking questions. The brain of the ADHD person needs time to process the question and the answer. The result is, overwhelming confusion that may end in anger.

For the most part I have a picture in my head and trying to explain it in any organized matter is a challenge. When I feel some pressures the challenge creates irritability and anxiousness. So my impulsive brain pushes me to just do it; throw myself into projects and tackle the minor details as they rise. But that leads to a disorganized mess, confusion and sometimes regret.

PROCRASTINATION

"Procrastination is a double edged sword," according to one of my clients and it can have a detrimental ripple effect. The truth is, many people who want other things to do or find something uninteresting, find every excuse to avoid a task at hand. Professionals suggest that people often take on too many responsibilities, and end up not being able to complete any of them. Then they keep putting things off until they are in a state of panic. They also spend too much time on the things that do not really matter and put off the things that really do matter (Robin, 1998).

Strategy: Use an area of strength as the motivator to avoid procrastination.

Depending on the personality type, some people need the competition to follow through on a task, others need incentives and rewards. Determine what the ADHD person naturally does in order to accomplish tasks they enjoy. I like challenges and I'm competitive; I race against time, and I like instant gratification. So I set a timer to fold laundry; I take a before picture of the laundry and I fold it, and then take an after picture. My gratification comes when I text the photo to a client. Certain motivators can make norepinephrine fire and this increases focus, and alertness. Procrastination also affects academics in a number of ways. I know when I was in my first year University, going out to a Halloween party the night before a mid-term seemed like it was a far better idea than staying home a doing some studying. I had little to no motivation to study. I had no idea that I needed to study as much as I did. I was pretty good at putting things off and doing something else, especially if something else was making good things fire in my brain. I always like to call it the feel good feelings, those neurotransmitters that I like; they just do what they need to for my brain. Studying and focusing just wasn't a priority for me. It always seemed to be so difficult and frustrating. It'll be a similar path for many children as they face challenges. Once again the neurotransmitters aren't firing and they can't plan ahead well enough, and they begin to feel panic and anxiety. I often share with parents my reflections on why I think children procrastinate. Imagine when a child is faced with a task that creates anxiety, frustration and tension, of course they're going to avoid it. We all know the natural reaction to stress and anxiety is avoidance or also known as procrastination.

DIFFICULTY PLANNING AHEAD

Difficulty planning ahead happens because some individuals lack the ability to maintain structure and organization in their mind. I naturally tend to be impulsive and do things at the last minute. Some people can only work well and stay focused when they're in a life or death situation, but it adds a lot of stress when a person has deadlines hanging over their head they never complete (Kustcher, 2007). I get caught up sometimes when I don't know what the end of a project looks like. I always need to see the end first and then go backwards. The truth is, the planning ahead is difficult, because I need a working model to go from. I know as I engage with several of my clients they're always mentioning the same issue. They have great ideas but can't manage to get them out, or even see any logic in the way to do things. It all becomes too overwhelming.

> **Strategy:** Create visual organizers that flow from one idea to another. Use flow charts; use bubble maps, or spider webbing strategies.

Many children with ADHD are visual learners as well as very kinesthetic and hands on. I like to visualize my plans using an idea of doing a puzzle; if I have a picture to go from at least I know what it is I'm trying to put together. I need to know what the end is. I believe it works the same for the ADHD brain. In order to plan ahead they need to know what the end is; then go back from there, and if there's gray areas expect delays and memory blocks.

IMPULSIVITY

Impulsivity or rushing to judgment is a problem that becomes increasingly serious over time. I'm one of those individuals that often needs things now. My impulsivities cause me to overlook crucial details; I become easily frustrated, and I become aggressive. My teachers always said, "You have sloppy handwriting, and make careless errors," this is a result of my need for instant gratification. My husband will often stop me in the middle of one of my impulsive projects and try to re direct me to focus on the finer details. However, the interruption of the flow of my impulsivities creates instant rage for me. Some people really don't understand what it's like to be inside my head. Too many teachers, colleagues, family and friends like to pass judgement on me as an ADHD person but in retrospect, I get things done.

I have ideas and they come to life; I have inspirations and I act on them.

Strategy: Don't blame the child; recognize there is a neurological impairment and manage it. Be aware of what triggers some of the impulsivities and avoid the incidents, activities or the environments. At the very least prepare for the triggers.

It's imperative to accept that people with an ADHD brain do function differently; it's primarily as a result of the executive delays in the brain.

HYPERACTIVITY

Hyperactivity is common with people with ADHD, but not everyone. A lot of people with ADHD are rather docile or even lethargic at times. Then at other times, they may be fidgety and overly talkative.

> **Strategy:** Learn an effective energy outlet that doesn't distract from performance, attention and focus. Use the tool as a tool not a toy. When it becomes a toy it's no longer effective.

I know there were times as I'd arrive at a Rugby practise and to be honest I was the energizing bunny. You know-- the one that just kept going and going and going. I reflect now, and I don't know how I managed to maintain a friendship. I really never processed much; I was always in a hurry and quite frankly, so full of energy I looked odd. I know and understand my characteristics now. I've educated myself and I make it my vocation to educate the other people in my life in order to manage my ADHD world. There is value in learning to advocate and explain that the ADHD brain is wired differently. I can advocate for myself and suggest my behaviors are a result of the lag in the frontal lobe of my brain where the executive functions are taking place. That sounds better than saying I don't really know why I'm hyper; I don't really know why I keep forgetting details, and I don't know why I yelled at them. Often in class or meetings I was so restless that eventually, I would just take a siesta. I looked bored because I was bored. I looked anxious because I had difficulty sitting still. I felt awkward; I never really had much to add to conversations and I found myself unable to sit long enough to enjoy a conversation unless it was about me.

EXECUTIVE FUNCTIONS

Research recently focuses on the executive functions of the frontal lobe of the brain. Executive functions are skills that scholarly literature refers to as brain based skills. These skills are required for people to execute or perform tasks.

Below is a collection of executive functioning skills that Russell Barkley uses to express the variety of tasks that the ADHD brain has difficulty with and or will experience a number of lags.

These are such things as:

Response inhibition: This helps with stopping and thinking before doing.

Working memory: This means remembering phone numbers, names, and directions.

Emotional control: So this means anger outbursts or meltdowns and excitable moments.

Sustained attention: Encourages listening and processing for longer periods of time.

Task initiation: Refers to getting started, or even knowing how to start or where to start.

Planning and prioritizing: This is big for getting assignments started and knowing how much time to spend on tasks, and then following through on those tasks.

Organization: Especially with too many things and not enough space, as well as clutter and other items that collect over time.

Time management: Not recognizing how much time has passed or what time it is, or how long it will take to get from point A to B, or even how long it will take to do a task.

Goal directed persistence: Following through on a task in order to move to the next task, motivation to just do it.

Flexibility: The ADHD brain needs plenty of time to process the transition from one task to another, process a change in plans, or the pressures of shifting tasks like shifting from Math to Science.

Meta cognition: Is self-talk and mindfulness and simply thinking it through based on past experiences. Perhaps a bit more like: seeing things from the perspective of a fly on the wall. In other words how others see us or hear us.

Children that have an ADHD diagnosis will often have a difficult time with emotional control. Some will actually display serious bouts of anger control issues.   A key executive function associated with emotional control is anger, an emotion that a lot people express. The frontal lobe of the brain is the area responsible for emotional control and anger. The ADHD brain is wired differently and anger has become a crucial characteristic for many to manage.

Strategy: Change the environment by reducing the sensory stimulation and the aggressive impulse will often pass.

People with ADHD tend to lose their temper; they have angry outbursts more often than their peers and family members (Robin, 1998). I remember a time when I was clearly overstimulated by a high pitched noise coming from the television that I grabbed for a hammer and smacked the T.V. The noise was gone but the T.V. had some permanent scars. As a result, my parents were pretty upset, and I really had no explanation for the meltdown. I was angry; I was mad, and I reached for the first thing I saw, and lashed out. I know now how to explain that moment, but sure didn't know then. Now I'd say, "I was oversensitive to the buzzing noise and became overstimulated." For most people that are hypersensitive, the overstimulation leads to irritation and then aggression. My aggressive outbursts are usually in the form of throwing things, lashing out, and needing something tactile to do with my hands.

When trying to understand behaviour of the ADHD person, people have to recognize that dealing with ADHD can be difficult on a number of levels. The ADHD person seems to have constant battles with defending their actions. They seem to always have to explain why, but the reality is they don't know why?

> **Strategy:** In order to begin to explain behaviours we need to understand what characteristic is being displayed; what triggered the behavior, and then manage it.

The diagnosis has a variety of characteristics to learn about. When people can understand what characteristic is interfering with success; then they might be able to manage some with strategies, and manage others with medication. At some point consulting a physician to determine if a medication might manage some of the characteristics is part of a treatment plan. The medication journey can be difficult and sometimes the side effects are far worse. Overtime a lot of people feel lost, anxious, and depressed; may also begin to battle the medication ups and downs. Many will end up self-medicating. Others become involved in dangerous sports, and dangerous business ventures or other deviant behaviors because they often lack focus or serenity. Others learn to manage and feel success. Many have self-reported that seeking activities that provide high stimulation sometimes works out successfully (Robin, 1998).

Strategy: Have a good understanding of ADHD medications and what the purpose of the medication is, and then determine what you need the medication to do. Are they drifty and dreamy, are they angry and aggressive, are they hyper and impulsive?

Students with ADHD often agree they are challenged with the diagnosis of ADHD, as well as the existing co-morbid behaviours.   According to research by Dr. Daniel Amen there are a number of co-morbidities associated with ADHD: procrastination, planning ahead, organizational issues, motivation, instant gratification, and a need for stimulation, forgetfulness, distractibility, impulsivity, poor time management, or the lack of self-esteem. ADHD is both a heterogeneous (affects both genders) and a pervasive disorder (interferes in all areas of life). Each child has a unique constellation of challenges. But, in all cases, multiple domains are affected (Whalen & Henker,1998).   According to the Learning Disabilities Association of Canada (LDAC) ADHD is recognized as a learning disability, and it also has a list of co-morbid behaviors that can interfere with academic and social awareness and success. Co-morbid disorders may have an impact on individuals with ADHD throughout their lives. It is estimated that at least 65% of children with ADHD have one or more co-morbid conditions. Other research also supports that several co-morbidities exist. For example, according to statistics from Harvard Medical School, 51% of people with ADHD have other serious disorders like conduct disorder, anxiety disorder or depression. LDAC also suggests these can be very serious problems that may end up becoming more serious than the ADHD. Learning disabilities are found in about 50% of people with ADHD. Many children face academic failure and are told that they are not living up to their potential. They have bursts of brilliance followed by poor performance, and it can be frustrating for teachers, parents and the children. They often have low self-esteem because they never quite live up to their true potential.

I believe troubled relationships and communication problems with family and friends are largely affecting the lives of people that struggle with their ADHD. Furthermore, as the ADHD child ages, they may often encounter a variety of relationship issues that can affect their self-esteem and well-being. I know I was the kind of child that had relationship and communication issues.

> **Strategy:** Teach young children appropriate social skills; help them understand behaviours and triggers for ADHD.

I'd get bored and start needing higher stimulation. I usually had the same problems every year at school because of boredom, distractibility, and impulsiveness. Often in conversations, I could say too much, and say it wrong; I become too loud or talk too intrusively. It was difficult for me to determine if the messages were received the intended way. Even now in conversations, I wonder if the other person is uncomfortable with what and how I said something.

LOWERED SELF ESTEEM

The lack of executive functioning skills can lead to serious social issues and a need for skills interventions in order to learn how to socialize with peers (Barkley, 2012). Low self-esteem is something that takes a toll on people because of the ADHD. Likely because the person has historically encountered situations where all anyone really notices is the negative; they point out the negative; they focus on the negative; and they reprimand for poor behavior. As a result, the child with ADHD feels somewhat less than their peers (Barkley, 2012).

> **Strategy:** Focus on what the student has completed versus what they haven't done; give constructive positive feedback, and then follow up with direct instructions. Tell them what to do next.

I know in the past most of my self-esteem issues were in social environments. I had such difficulty processing conversations; processing news, and even the information people were presenting. I never understood the depth of a conversation or the value in one. I couldn't focus and process long enough to recognize any interest in the topic. So, I didn't add much to conversations. I didn't like playing trivial pursuit; I couldn't sit still long enough to play games and I despised having to do group work. But, most of all I regret that I was **tuned out** for most of my undergrad at University.

TIME MANAGEMENT AND MOTIVATION

According to lectures by Barkley (September 2012), time management and motivation are also affected. The lack of motivation in people with ADHD happens when people know they need to get started, and they know they need to get going, but just cannot seem to do it. Motivation begins with having a goal, a focus, and then determining what encourages them to do it. The ADHD child needs supports and strategies in order to learn how to manage and succeed (Lavoie, 2007).

> **Strategy:** Use timers and time limits; set a time for the end result, or the completion of a task. Not being aware of time creates a number of unfavorable situations. It can also be a motivator for some.

Most people recognize how long it takes to get from A to B or how long it takes to complete an assignment, or a project; how long it will be, and what you need to do. People with ADHD are really oblivious to many tasks that require a time constraint. Just recently I was leaving for Arizona for a business conference and the morning of the flight I was painting a dresser, building a shelf, recovering a chair and painting the headboard to match the dresser. Then suddenly I looked up and WOW where did the time go? My husband came crashing through the door hysterical because I was supposed to be packing and getting ready to leave. All kinds of questions flying, what are you doing, why aren't you packing, what's going on, where's your bags, why aren't you dressed? Well, I looked at him, and I said, "Oh Gosh, I lost track of time".

ANXIETY AND DEPRESSION

Furthermore, individuals that struggle with ADHD will often have anxiety and depression as co-morbidities that accompany the diagnosis. Anxiety is the body's response to a stressor. For those with ADHD, that response occurs more often, in more situations, and definitely becomes an inhibiting factor. It is triggered by a situation and the response can impact their life negatively (Barkley, 2012). Feelings of overwhelming sadness, despair, and despondency, may affect overall performance (Kutscher, 2007).

Strategy: Learn how to identify situations that create anxiety and then develop some coping methods in order to manage the anxious moment.

Psychologists from The Learning Disabilities Association of Saskatchewan suggest children with ADHD may experience more failures, anxiety, stress, anger issues, and self-esteem problems than others, and in the end the ADHD may become debilitating. However with the appropriate interventions there can be success. I realize how valuable an assessment with the appropriate diagnosis is. I was diagnosed with exam anxiety. I never understood why people were done so early, why they'd get up and go so fast. I was always so mad because people were turning pages and making noises. But, it was me, my senses were always heightened on the days of exams because I was so anxious and nervous; always predicting failures and catastrophizing the results, and then distorting everything. My ADHD has had a significant impact on my academic achievements; personal goals and outcomes.

"I know now, that I'm not stupid, lazy or dumb. It just takes me time to process, and I need to tap into all of my senses." I learn using a variety of kinesthetic strategies that increase my focus, attention and reduce my distractibility. And, these days I push for accommodations because I know it benefits me in so many ways."

~Christina Johnson-Quan

THE EXECUTIVE

FUNCTIONING EFFECTS ON

BEHAVIOUR AND LEARNING

Stand up to your obstacles

and do something about them.

You will find that they haven't

half the strength you think they

have.

~Norman Vincent Peale

I mentioned earlier, the significant impact on the executive functions of the ADHD brain in the frontal lobe. To summarize and explain the effect of executive functions we can conclude that the executive functioning comprises of at least six components, according to Arthur L. Robin (2010). He suggests the six components are a combination of several behavioural inhibitions, and these inhibitions can have a lifelong impact on many people, including parents and teachers closely associated with the diagnosis. These behavioural inhibitions affect working memory (recalling dates, numbers, and addresses) verbal working memory (words, names, directions, and information), self-regulation (emotional control, tone, volume, and body language) and motor control resulting in a combination of abnormal behaviours. Many of us who struggle with ADHD have a multitude of characteristics. I don't think we plan to be a mess; or plan to have the "I don't care attitude," but things are happening so fast. I know I move onto the next thing before I've accomplished the last. Or maybe I just get bored and need to move on. Sometimes I even tune out. When I'm tuned out and someone startles me, I respond impulsively; sometimes becoming oppositional, and I usually end up feeling anxious and irritated. One of the things to acknowledge about children with ADHD is: they do things differently, and will often refuse to listen to the lecture, then tune out after the first couple of minutes. I can flashback to a time when I was around 12, and my father used to say to me over and over again, "Christina, why can't you just do it like this." Years later, I realize I just didn't get it his way; he saw things differently than I did. As a result I would often become oppositional or confrontational, and withdraw. Research indicates that in real life experiences people with ADHD may become oppositional and defiant more than their school age counterparts (Barkley, 2006).

> **Strategy:** Believe in the validity of the diagnosis and understand the diagnosis creates characteristics; work with it, not against it.

In **my** homework world, situations always became oppositional and confrontational. My perspective on things was always from a different angle, and my father didn't realize that I learned differently. He would go on and on and on, and I tuned out after the first word. My drifty, dreamy was always kicking in, especially because of his tone of voice. It happens all the time in my world, and I see it in the faces of people as they drift and dream and, in the words of a girl I know with ADHD, "go to the moon." My strategy to parents is: they need to say things using simple terms; language and phrases the child understands, and they need to keep things short. Because, by the time they have talked on for a couple minutes, the ADHD brain is thinking about something else. I coach parents as well, because in order for them to realize what it's like for children to live with ADHD, they need knowledge too.

Now picture this: Going down the highway the wrong way, with cars flying past you, honking their horns; and all you see is a blur. That's often what it's like to have ADHD. Then add sensitivity to sounds and anxiety, plus other characteristics. There's a lot going on. I began to educate myself about ADHD; to educate others, in order to move on in life. I believe, as we learn more about the impact ADHD has on the lives of others, we can eventually determine what makes the ADHD brain tick. Overtime, it seems that many people with ADHD begin to internalize their emotions and externalize their anger and energy. Despite the negative impact of the characteristics of ADHD, few systematic efforts have targeted these problems in children (Abitkoff et al., 2001). "I could be the research", because I was one of those children that began to externalize my emotions. I became angry and frustrated and easily irritated and then overstimulated. More often than not, I was distracted and in my drifty dreamy world. Then when people would yell to get my attention, then I would become angry, and lash out.

"I know being overstimulated can

create feelings of anxiety for me,

leading to anger, irritation and

impulsive, uncontrollable lashing out."

~Christina Johnson-Quan

MULTIMODAL TREATMENT

I believe that everything happens for

a reason. People change so

that you can learn to let go,

things go wrong so that

you appreciate them when they're right,

you believe lies so you eventually learn

to trust no one but yourself,

and sometimes good things fall apart so

better things can fall together.

~Marilyn Monroe

The most common treatments for children and adolescents with ADHD include medication and behavior modification strategies implemented across home and their school settings. The underlying treatment for ADHD is called a multimodal approach (Plumer & Stoner , 2005). It involves the collaboration of several caring individuals and other team members with the same goals and visions. Goldstein and Naglieri (2008) suggest that medication, education, as well as behavioral and environmental management are vital in a long-term strategic plan for managing ADHD. Doctors, psychologists and specialists indicate that one intervention alone may not deal with the full range of characteristics that interfere with success for students with ADHD. There is likely a need for a combination of therapies and a collection of multi-modal treatments. Overall, the literature for treatments involving family counselling, behavioral intervention, and academic techniques suggest that none of these strategies are sufficient on their own. If fact, each type of intervention targets different areas of impairment.

Strategy: Educate as many people as you can about ADHD and the impact on you or your child.

Research suggests a combination of treatments may be necessary to address the co-morbid characteristics of students with ADHD. The ADHD child can learn how to manage their self-discipline as well as their self-regulation skills. But they need to be taught what triggers behaviours and they need to learn how to apply a strategy. ADHD is a disorder that is managed not cured. The child diagnosed with ADHD will likely benefit from knowing their diagnosis exists and then understanding how it impacts them in a number of different environments. But, who teaches the child about their ADHD? I believe anyone who engages with children that have a diagnosis needs to become an expert on the characteristics, the behaviors and understand the diagnosis in order to encourage personal growth.

"The best part of my current success and management of ADHD is education. I made it my vocation to teach myself anything and everything about ADHD. I use medication to manage the overstimulation and anger, and I have mastered the art of creating strategies."

~Christina Johnson-Quan

THE BENEFITS OF A PROPER

DIAGNOSIS IN LEARNING

COPING STRATEGIES

Individuals, who cultivate a

variety of skills seem brighter,

more energetic and more

adaptable than those who know

how to do one thing only.

~Robert Shea

My recent diagnosis helps describe the journey and the debilitating effects of ADHD. I quit job after job, found myself in serious debt, lost, disheveled and in severe states of angst. I'm hypersensitive to noises, smells, touch and light, all of which affect me every day. I'm in a constant state of turmoil and reflection, as I attempt to manage my characteristics. Without my medication and coping strategies, I look like I feel. I become overstimulated, unable to manage and, as a result, I can become impulsive and don't function well. Does ADHD affect my daily life? Of course it does. Do you get up every day and see the light at the end of the tunnel? I don't! I just pray to get through another day. Imagine driving down the highway at night in a snowstorm with your headlights on bright and all you see are snowflakes while looking at your dashboard and seeing ten T.V. stations on at once. But that's not it; you realize you're on the wrong side of the road as cars speed towards you honking their horns. Education becomes a form of coping in order to understand the impact ADHD has on the lives of people that live with the diagnosis, as well as for those that have to live with others with a diagnosis.

> **Strategy:** Get professional assistance in order to be able to create strategies that encourage positive lifelong changes. Having a variety of coping strategies are effective interventions in order to manage successfully.

I realize the diagnosis will never go away and it will never change, but now as an educated adult I can change; learn to manage and advocate for myself. But who advocates for children? As I flashback, I remember a phrase that so many educators, coaches, and people would say to me, "Christina we need a thinker." That didn't make any sense to me. I do think, I think all the time. One of things that people with ADHD have is this ability to think, over think, and think again. Some call it rumination; some call it distracted, and some call it obsessing over things that are simple to others. Socially, I often misinterpret certain information, conversations or instructions. I used to think as a child that everything I did was wrong, or bad, or I'd be in trouble. When teachers would say, "Christina, listen to me the first time, I'm not repeating myself." Or my parents would say, "You bad girl, you shouldn't do that." I realize now that my actions and my behaviours are significantly different from the person I am. I remember times when the teacher would say: "Pass your papers back;" I thought they said, "Pat your neighbours back." So I did what I thought the teacher said, I'd pat my neighbours back, and guess what? I'd be in trouble trotting to the principal's office. But was I a bad person? No, but I always thought I did something really wrong. The truth is, when they'd ask me what I did wrong, I never knew; I really thought I was doing what I was told. Eventually, I thought everything I did was bad. Sometimes, as the teacher was standing in the front of the class, I'd look and start counting the wrinkles in their pants: 45, 46, 47. Am I easily distractible? Sure am, as I would shake my head; blink my eyes and realize I had missed the last ten minutes as well as the assignment. Like many other children who appear lost, I was lost, and then I'd lean over to ask someone. Then **BANG** in trouble again. The distractibility is something I call the drifty/ dreamy. It's a nice little siesta, the daydream. The ADHD brain is wired differently and I've had to change my thinking and recognize I have a different hard wiring than others. I can sometimes get this glazed over look in my eyes; I'm actually in a deep relaxed state where the delta brainwaves are affected and this interferes with focus. So that's who I am, but who I am is affected everyday by my neurological impairment; without the medications, strategies and education, who knows where I'd be. Throughout my journey, I've learned that not everyone's brain is wired the same; some of us get information differently, retrieve it differently, and store it differently. Others are more sensitive, empathetic and emotional. I have also learned I'm different, but I'm not stupid, lazy or dumb. Current feedback from parents of students with learning disabilities through The Learning Disabilities Association of Saskatchewan (LDAS) suggest that children are continually being assessed and diagnosed but there are no opportunities for certain recommendations to be fulfilled because of the lack of services available in the schools. ADHD is a widely known and discussed topic in schools today and there are a number of alternative treatments. There are a variety of studies that evaluate the impact of non-medicated treatment interventions and the findings reveal that both traditional and non-traditional treatments are effective. That being said, interventions at an early age may be effective in helping children with ADHD to understand the impact it has on their outcome academically.

"Intervention and early

education is important for

overall success. I believe

educators and parents need to

be knowledgeable about the

nature of the disorder and the

strategies."

~Christina Johnson-Quan

A COLES NOTES ON DISTRACTIBILITY AND THE IDENTIFICATION OF THRESHOLD AND TRIGGERS

Life isn't about waiting for

the storm to pass...

It's about learning to Dance in

the Rain.

~Vivian Greene

My parents had patience but there was a breaking point for them much like any parent. However, they didn't know about my threshold or my triggers, and I didn't know my threshold and triggers either.

> **Strategy:** Develop a variety of self-awareness skills. Learn what interferes with success and then learn what the limit is before the serious meltdown occurs.

I can imagine things may have been different if only we had some information; we knew some coping strategies or some education about impulsivities and distractibility. If only there had been a teacher that could recognize my needs, maybe even a teacher that had compassion and empathy for my learning style. If only my ADHD had been identified, then teachers could have explored the characteristics of ADHD, and they could have learned how to help me through the ADHD moments. My parents could have understood the impact of medications, and they could have realized there were strategies I could use. I know that over the years, I could have used a mentor. Now, as an adult, I want to help others with ADHD, and I want to be their mentor. I always believe in them because I'm one of them. Attaining success starts with children recognizing they aren't stupid, lazy or dumb. They may be a bit distracted and might have missed some key information. I want children with ADHD to learn to ask themselves, "What is happening right now, and what can I do about it?" I've learned that an ADHD moment is preceded by a variety of triggers. Basically I ask myself, what is it that's setting off the behavior? What is interfering with the child's success in the classroom? There is a significant risk for children with ADHD to face a number of challenges in the classroom. They may not directly have a learning disability, but the troubles they encounter as a result of the lag in their executive functioning capacity may interfere with their academic success. Therefore, there needs to be appropriate assessments, diagnosis and interventions. The Diagnostic Statistical Manual (DSM) labels Attention Deficit Hyperactivity Disorder (ADHD or AD/HD or ADD) as a neurobehavioral developmental disorder. The DSM –V, 2009 is a reliable tool that allows psychologists to screen children for at-risk behaviours that are fundamental characteristics of ADHD. The core characteristics are inattention, impulsivity, and excessive motor activity (Whalen & Henker, 1998).

In my case I'm often distracted; I'm drifty, dreamy and deep in my own thoughts. I recognize I need to focus, and every day I need to tell myself over and over again things like, "Christina, what should you be doing right now? "Christina, stop and think." So, as an educator and a coach, I'm encouraging children to figure out how to fix their ADHD moment and determine their problem by reflecting.

> **Strategy:** Encourage reflection on the moment; their feelings, the situation, and the outcomes. Be creative in developing interventions and strategies then modify, reflect, and be consistent.

But, as a journey of self-discovery, this has to be done in a positive way; by encouraging and respecting that each child can develop increased self-awareness. Otherwise the journey is faced with opposition and defiance because like me and many others, feelings of anxiety and intimidation start to interfere. It's hard to identify but that's how most ADHD children feel. I know for me as an adult diagnosed with ADHD, if the wrong tone is used or the wrong body language, I interpret everything wrong and sometimes end up in a panic attack. Regardless of the treatment or the multimodal approaches used, the underlying strategy remains the same: treatment needs to be multi-modal. Note: that multi-modal is a process that involves understanding the diagnosis of ADHD through education, supports, and strategies. Then, applying strategies, and possibly using a pharmaceutical intervention in order to be able to manage. Suggestions from Goldstein and Naglieri, (2008) suggest the premise in managing problems associated with ADHD falls on the individual because the individual must learn how to manage their self-discipline as well as their self-regulation skills. Strategy: Develop an effective means of positive self-talk that stimulates, and motivates changes through increased accountability. I got to thinking of something, and of course it struck me too late, but this was an ADHD moment. One day in late September I was driving to work and decided I needed to chomp on my finger nail. You know when you get that little hang nail, that piece of skin that just bothers you? I was hyper focused on tearing at my skin on my finger; I figured I can multi task, right? I need to get this little piece of skin that jagged nail, that little dry flap and just tug a little and have it gone. But in order to do that I needed to use both hands to grab that piece of skin, so I could grind at it with my teeth. So I decided to drive with my knee while I chomped and ground at that piece of skin. Oh! And by the way there was this guy walking over the overpass near the PAC building; the wind was blowing just right to catch the beautiful fall leaves and I watched as they circled around him like a colony of bees protecting their hive. He caught my attention too. But in the middle of all that, I stopped and said to myself, "OK, Christina what are you doing right now? What should you be doing?" So I turned off the radio, stopped chomping on my nail and focused on one thing, **DRIVING.** I do more self-talk, in order to manage the chaos of multi-tasking. At this moment while I was driving I said, "Do one thing, then the other; stop hyper focusing on the nails, get focused and DRIVE!" According to an article published in the *Italian Journal of Pediatrics* by Paolo Curatolo, Elisa D'Agati, and Romina Moavero (2010) we note that:

> "Individuals with ADHD present difficulties in several domains of attentional and cognitive functions: problem solving, planning, orienting, alerting, cognitive flexibility, sustained attention, response inhibition, and working memory. Other domains involving affective components, such as motivation and delay aversion, are also affected. Motor difficulties, such as problems with sensory motor coordination

including poor handwriting, clumsiness, and marked delays in achieving motor milestones, have also been reported and the prevalence of motor impairment in the ADHD population has been estimated to be approximately 50%."

"In order to manage any of the characteristics of ADHD, a person has to know what's creating their behavior or what's triggering it, then they can STOP and THINK, and APPLY a strategy."

~Christina Johnson-Quan

TRANSITIONS AND ENVIRONMENTAL CHANGES "HEY I WAS, LOOK IT'S A BIRD"

> If you aren't in the moment,
>
> you are either looking forward to
>
> uncertainty,
>
> or back to pain and regret.
>
> ~Jim Carrey

Sometimes I get to thinking about something, and of course get to thinking about something else and then something else. One might say, "Welcome to the life of a person with ADHD." It seems that one thought ripples into another; then another rippled thought and then suddenly the realization that I never got anything accomplished.

Strategy: Give the ADHD child the gift of time. Recognize children who struggle with ADHD are often challenged with an inability to transition well, and the child won't be able to explain why?

Another term used to identify with transitions is concept shifting. Concept shifting is the ability to regulate one's own behavior or to shift a course of thought or action according to the demands of the situation (Marchetta, Hurks, and Jolles, 2008). The research also shows that individuals with ADHD will often display characteristics that are co-morbid behaviours (depression, oppositional defiance, OCD) as a result of the concept shift or transition. These problems with shifting from one concept to another and with self-control have also been reported in clinical practice as complaints relating to the failure to organize and complete activities. (Marchetta, Hurks, and Jolles, 2008).

Reflecting on transitions, I remember a time just recently with my three year old son. He was busy doing a puzzle; I yanked him up and told him we had to go to daycare. It was time to leave; I needed to get them in the car, buckled in, and out of our neighbourhood before 8:25 AM or I'd be stuck in traffic. He threw a tantrum, had a meltdown. So do children like transition? When given plenty of warning transitions are simplified. Without the warning, we get the meltdown. We all need time to process change.

One of the keys to the diagnosis of ADHD is recognizing that the characteristics are present for everyone, but for those with ADHD the characteristics interfere, are prolonged, and happen in multiple areas of a person's life. For people with ADHD there seems to be a lack of time sense, or priority, even motivation. But I learned from my three year old to recognize that children probably won't like it too much if they're forced to change right now. Parents may find that family members refuse to care for the child, and that other children do not invite them to parties or out to play. Relationships and communication can affect the ADHD person's behaviour.

Strategy: Learn to create an environment that enables positive modes of communication. Poor communication affects behaviours.

Behaviour can be affected by interrupted sleep, or poor sleep habits. Many children with ADHD have poor sleep patterns, and although they appear not to need much sleep, daytime behaviour is often worse when sleep is deprived (Harpen, 2005).

Strategy: Monitor sleep patterns and mood. Some situations may require stricter evening routines to wind down, or even a simple additive such as melatonin.

I didn't sleep well; I was often on the go and I didn't like being told what to do. Which reminds me of a time when I was quite young. It was an event that triggered a nasty meltdown and often ended in behaviours my parents couldn't manage. I was out at the park on one of those climbing frames shaped like a dome. Once you get to the top, you're the king of the castle. I know my mother always told me, "Be careful", but sometimes I'd be distracted. So there we were, at the park and someone yelled, "OK time to go." Well I was looking out at the sunset; not really processing much. I was gazing at the beautiful orange and yellow colors that spread over the sky, and the shadows of the birds as they swooped in the air. Then suddenly, I heard this awful sounding screech, "C H R I S T I N A!" I fell straight down; cracked my head, blood spewing and rocks embedded in my forehead. Well, at least that's what I remember. I looked up and there was a lady trying to help me, but I wasn't about to go anywhere. I was at the park, playing; watching the sun set, and it wasn't time to go. Then I had a meltdown. The meltdown is likely the most difficult transition to deal with as a parent. In order to understand situations and what triggers behaviours, I reflect on moments like the previous one with a number of my clients. Research suggests children with ADHD will likely do better with transitions when given plenty of time to prepare for change. I think my mother often thought I was trying to mess things up. But, now I can advocate for myself and explain that I wasn't trying to mess up her day. I was just experiencing difficulty transitioning. I know as a parent and as an educator for children with ADHD, I want to help them reflect; understand their ADHD, and manage it. After all, it takes one to know one.

"Note to self: if they look confused

and look like they don't know what's

going on, they probably are confused

and don't know, so just help them."

~Christina Johnson-Quan

COPING STRATEGIES; SUPPORTS FOR LEARNING DISABILITIES AND CHALLENGES. "SHOULDN'T SCHOOL BE FUN?"

When you have to cope with a lot of

problems,

you're either going to sink or you're

going to swim.

~ Tom Cruise

I recently had some flashbacks of my school experience. It was difficult, full of frustration, tension and a lot of anger. My parents didn't understand me; my teachers were disappointed with my lack of follow through and effort. I guess now, years later, I have empathy for children that have ADHD because I was there.

> **Strategy:** Recognize a need for interventions; look for help, find professionals, and seek alternative instruction and accommodations.

Now, I'm getting the support I need. Richard Lavoie (2007), the author of *The Motivation Breakthrough*, suggests that a child's education is affected by four relationships. These four relationships are: relationships with classmates, relationships with teachers, their relationships with their parents, and their parents' relationship with the teacher. So how does that resonate with me? I'm educating others, and I'm teaching youth how to advocate for themselves while sharing experiences with students and parents, and trying to bridge a gap between home and school. So I got to thinking about how little some of our teachers really know about children that struggle with ADHD. Recently I was working with this precious little girl. She came into my office so excited and so bouncy; she had morning hair. You know that bump in your hair that happens when you sleep on your head wrong? So we started to talk about school and why and how she struggles. She said to me her teacher stands still too much, and it causes her to go to the moon. She often drifts away for a whole lesson if the teacher isn't moving. So here's this brilliant little girl that misses whole lessons because she becomes 'hypnotized' when her teacher stands still. It's not that she doesn't get it; not interested, but it's the teacher's teaching style. It seems many people believe that, if the student tries harder or if they pay more attention, they'll get it. The truth is they might need some accommodations or they may need some modifications; even a different approach to be able to grasp concepts. A lot of children who struggle with ADHD also have some learning issues. **The one goal I have is: To be able to help parents understand their child, in order for their child to have success and feel positive about their academic experience.**

Strategy: Involve the student in positive experiences in the classroom by asking them direct questions; probing them in a positive way and believing in them. This builds their self-esteem.

Had my parents known more about disabilities they could have advocated for accommodations? I encourage educating yourself as best you can. Whether you're the person with ADHD or it's your child that has the diagnosis; even if you're the teacher that has to work with a student with ADHD—educate yourself. I came across an amazing reference called Try On Learning Disabilities (TOLD). It's an easy read that helps identify characteristics of disabilities and also suggests a number of strategies. Parent's need to be the voice for their child, they need to advocate, and they need to educate themselves. I wish my parent's understood the value of a Personal Program Plan (PPP), and I can imagine a personal plan might have encouraged greater success for me. I believe parents need to communicate with teachers about effective strategies and interventions. I can only imagine if my parents had been involved with the school to implement strategies in my learning environment. I reflect now and then about the value parents can have on planning for success. I knew I needed help, but there wasn't a lot of knowledge about ADHD in 1980 and I didn't know how to ask for help, or even what to ask about. After many conversations and consults with a variety of professionals, and students I discovered I'm not unusual. There's a variety of people that have the diagnosis; some were diagnosed at a young age, some in their youth and others as adults. The reality is, the underlying characteristics of the diagnosis are different for everyone but the long term consequences are very similar.

"I realize the value in helping students and children with ADHD. I know that so many teachers and parents use those throw away lines that some people forget but the ADHD child they hold that little comment in their memory forever. So let go of comparing the ADHD child to everyone else, because they need the help, they need attention, they need direct instruction, and the best gift you can give them is TIME."

~Christina Johnson-Quan

ANXIETY: A NASTY CHARACTERISTIC AFFECTING ADHD CHILDREN

Anxiety does not empty tomorrow of

its sorrow...

but only empties today of

its strength.

~ C. H. Spurgeon

For some people starting something knew or something different is motivating. For others it can be a rippling affect that turns to anxiety. For me every week is another one of those weeks. Manic Mondays seem to start like that. I guess it has its name for a reason, especially if you've been in holiday mode. Just imagine how children feel. What was routine for sleeping in and hanging around is now back to some of the pressures and anxieties they experience at school. Most people who struggle with ADHD also have some kind of anxiety. In some cases, it's interfering with daily life; in other cases, not so much.

Strategy: Learn how to identify anxiety and learn how to create coping strategies in order to manage.

I remember chewing my nails, tapping my pencil and playing a tune with my toes. I have so many holes in my socks! I think our role as adults and parents is to understand where those anxieties are coming from in order to help others understand anxiety as well. It's important for others to recognize how the person with ADHD is reacting, or how they express anxiety. So I have to ask myself now: Is it because I was angry, frustrated and worked up; defensive, or withdrawn? I know I'm all of the above in many situations. But, did I know it five years ago; did I understand it; and did I recognize the impact or even know I was feeling anything? In order to help children who struggle with their anxiety, I need to understand how it manifests itself and explore with children how they express their anxieties. So I observe and I probe in order to help them understand their anxiety. One of my clients, he was a grade 9 boy from Asquith. He talked about his apprehensions in school. Inside my mix of characteristics that interfere with my success I'm understanding, approachable, empathetic, and a good listener. I'm also exceptional at probing. He expressed the confusion and frustrations he experienced just before exams and quizzes. He said he starts to chew his nails and scratch his face; his heart races and he starts to sweat. He can't even think and, his classmates seem to be turning pages so loud that's all he can hear. Later that week I emailed his teachers and disclosed his anxiety; now he gets a quiet room and extra time. I shared with his teachers and his parents, the understanding that: there is no easy fix for ADHD or the co morbid characteristics and behaviours. Furthermore, I expressed how his anxiety interferes with his success. It can impair performance in cognitive functions including attention, memory, concept formation as well as problem solving.   Anxiety impacts people in a number of different ways.

In my ADHD world I can recognize my anxiety as part of daily life, and a result of experiencing new or unfamiliar events, places and people. Situations arise every day that can test my nerves, and sometimes I'm motivated by that feeling of being 'on the edge.' For me there's an interaction with task difficulty. Anxiety can result in poorer performance in complex tasks, but may improve performance on very simple tasks. In many situations, anticipation (which is an anxiety symptom for me) sharpens other senses and causes a hyper-alert state of mind which helps me accomplish the task.   But depending on the circumstances, it can also be a catastrophe because I'm overstimulated and overwhelmed.   For others, the anxiety symptoms are not only unwelcome, but also alarming and to be avoided at all costs. Anxiety can be an inhibiting factor in learning and therefore has received considerable attention. It is closely related to arousal, attention and motivation as well as emotions. Anxiety is usually triggered by a situation that involves a decision or judgment. Tests and exams are common situations that create anxiety in educational settings (Barkley, 2008). There's a constant mantra I express to families: In order to manage ADHD the treatment needs to be multi-modal. But, people have to learn to manage with coping strategies, education and supports.

"I've discovered there are a number of situations where I'm making predictions, distorting situations and often never seeing the positives. I even can go so far as to say, as much as I love exercise the anticipation of the event and the formal competition creates anxiety for me."

~Christina Johnson-Quan

IMPULSIVITY: DID I REALLY DO THAT AGAIN?

Where one person shapes their life

by precept and example,

there are a thousand who have

shaped it by impulse and

circumstances.

~James Russell Lowell

Have you ever just watched children play; then ask yourself why some play well together and some just don't? So here's the situation: I was watching two children play. They were interacting, and I was hovering around the corner. I knew these two boys. One has ADHD and the other doesn't. So the child with ADHD sees his friend with a toy he wants, so he whacks the other little boy and takes it. Then he looks around and likely thinks "Did anyone see me?" So I got to thinking about impulsivities and the impact, and the whys and why nots? So reverse that situation: the boy without ADHD wants the other little boy's toy. So he looks around, whacks his little friend, and takes his toy. The biggest difference in these two situations seems to be impulsivity. As we investigate what impulsivity means, research suggests that impulsivity is connected to behavioral inhibitions. Inhibitions are associated with a series of cognitive processes by which a planned response may be delayed or withheld, or an on-going response to something may be interrupted (Carroll et al, 2011). To review the situation, the first little ADHD child doesn't understand the consequences of his actions, nor can he plan that far ahead to even be able to justify his actions. So the other little boy is fully aware that if someone is watching, he'll get into trouble. I can be more aware now, I realize the triggers, and I think this situation is a good example of understanding impulsivities and ADHD.

Strategy: Acknowledge the behaviour and redirect them towards a more positive behavior that demonstrates self-control.

> **Strategy:** Don't ask the ADHD person, why they did what they did. They won't know, but instead I think it's valuable to realize that people with ADHD will be impulsive and not be able to explain why.

Learn to accept the behaviors as a characteristic of their ADHD. I believe we have to try and teach children to slow down and think about what might happen. Help them to problem solve before it becomes the problem, because the more anger we muster up in children with ADHD the more opposition the child likely expresses.

"I know now, I wish I could have been better at controlling myself, but the truth is, if you tell me what to do, rather then what not to do. I'll do it. Redirect with direct instruction. I'm like a soldier; give me black and white, no gray areas. I'll do it."

~Christina Johnson-Quan

ORGANIZATIONAL SKILLS:

ME AND HIM, WHAT's THE

DIFFERENCE AND WHY?

I've always done 20 things at once.

It's my way of staying alive, not to

keep one dish cooking,

but several dishes going.

And I'm pretty organized.

~ Patrice Leconte

It's a tough road! I know, because I've traveled it, and it does get better. But, before it gets better, I think most people with ADHD have some kind of revelation. I know for me it happened when I hit rock bottom. That's a story for another time. My revelation happened when I was 39; for some reason all the nagging from my parents suddenly made sense.

Strategy: Educate don't preach. Guided discovery helps children with ADHD learn acceptable behaviors. Preaching and yelling at them, makes them oppositional. Helping them understand their ADHD and teaching strategies, encourages growth.

My personal experiences, my research and greater understanding of myself, have enlightened me, to be able to connect my behaviors to a characteristic.

I've learned I need to be accountable and manage myself better.

So here's my situation. I was looking at my side of the room the other day and I thought what's wrong with this picture? My clothes are piled up; my laundry is sitting in a heap; and my six slippers are scattered everywhere. My husband's side of the room: clothes are neatly stacked; no laundry in a heap but in a small laundry basket; slippers; just one pair are neatly tucked under his stool where his folded pajamas sit. So, what's my problem? I decided its accountability and instant gratification. Suddenly I figured it out. For years, as my parents told me what to do, I thought they were being bossy, controlling and nosey. In retrospect I realize they were trying to help me to be accountable. I can reflect on my experiences now and recognize the impact my ADHD has. So I began to explore strategies on reaching children with a positive, encouraging tone that increases follow through. My strategy is to communicate with children with ADHD without sounding bossy, controlling or nosey, and yet still encourage them to be accountable. I think more about accountability now. I guess it's because I'm not as self-centred and I'm more willing to accept feedback from others. My role as a coach is to develop stronger communication skills and greater understanding. I help children to help themselves by observing and responding, in order to create some positive lifelong changes.

"So instead of telling children what they're always doing wrong, I give them direct instruction on what to do. I try to probe them to self-discover alternatives, and then determine what better behaviour is and what acceptable behaviour is."

~Christina Johnson-Quan

PROCRASTINATION

Procrastination is the art of keeping up

with yesterday.

~ *Don Marquis*

I know, and you know, it's the same thing over and over again: "I'll do it...I'll do it...." Have you ever wondered why some people never quite finish something? Or even if they do finish it, it's kind of messy and not really done well. Things are sort of rushed and not their best effort?

> **Strategy:** Learn about the neurotransmitters in the brain and understand how they fire. Recognize the value in knowing what the brain is missing; what it needs and how to get the brain firing.

For me it's all about instant gratification. My need for instant gratification gets in the way of follow through, and it drives my procrastination. The need for the end now, and the need to see the end before I even know what the other parts look like is overwhelming. So what does that really mean? It means that I know there are better ways to do things.

I know there are faster ways to get it done, and I like the rewards. So why is it I never quite work up to my potential? Why is it my parents always pushed me further, harder, and wondered why I couldn't follow through? Maybe it's motivation; maybe it's not understanding the process, and maybe even fear or procrastination, but I'm pretty sure it's not because I was lazy or stupid. I know my parents asked the same things over and over. They would always tell teachers how I'm a great starter, but never quite follow through. So now I ask myself, "What ADHD characteristic is interfering with success?" I'll tell you why I was a classic procrastinator: *There's always something better to do.* It would be futile to do what someone else or others expect me to do and besides, someone else would likely do it better. Procrastination seems to be a combination of characteristics which makes it even harder to work on. It's not just one characteristic, but it's a few.

Don't get me wrong though; there's a lot of creativity in the ADHD brain, and sometimes I can be hyper-focussed, and do an amazing job. I can be artistic and so talented, but what's getting in the way of finishing or even starting? It's a number of issues; some might say lazy, or inconsiderate. But the truth is there's more to it than that. I have a combination of lags in my executive functioning skills. There's also anxiety, and processing issues that interfere with my success. If only my parents, my brother and my friends, were more sensitive with the whys and why nots, things may have turned out differently.

In my early teaching days I would see children that were so terribly isolated. My hope as an advocate and an ADHD coach is to help children feel less isolated, by helping them understand the characteristics, and understand behaviours. So now, many years later, after a long journey of self-discovery, I help them to figure out what it is that's getting in the way of them getting it done. Then I encourage them to solve the problem by using coping strategies that will work for them. As someone who has lived with undiagnosed ADHD, and recently discovered **_MESS,_** I have to ask myself, "What is it that's getting in the way?" This is a coping strategy that evolved for me. Stop and think and ask myself questions. It seems to work. I often have to self-talk in order to manage the moment and recognize what's happening. Then I need to apply a coping strategy in order to succeed.

In my profession, I have opportunities to work daily with clients of all ages who are diagnosed with ADHD. Clients often arrive for treatment with their own explanatory narratives. The narrative themes often reflect strong negative feelings about their experiences such as inadequacy or failure. Research in some areas suggests that the nature of these beliefs is this: an individual makes life decisions based on assumptions, past experiences, and false validity. In essence I recognize the same patterns for myself. I also know that my catastrophizing is a result of my anxieties. For example, a woman might avoid taking a computer course that could help her advance in her job because she defines herself as a horrible student on the basis of the difficulties she had in high school (Ramsy, 2002). When I decide that doing something is my goal then doing it becomes easier and the motivation can shift. When situations seem forceful I recognize I become oppositional and argumentative until my motivation declines, and then I procrastinate. The research in areas about procrastination tends to indicate that people will respond better with positive incentives, with rewards and with instant gratification (Barkley, 2012).

What does it all mean? Why share stories of life, of failures and expectations, of beliefs and values? I wonder about the impact on others. I wonder about educating teachers and parents regarding strategies, and about being more sensitive. I wonder about being more self-aware of tone and incentives offered through positive words and feedback. I wonder if others might be able to recognize how to get people with ADHD to respond, to advocate about their ADHD issues, and to look for signs of an ADHD moment. I wonder how much it might help if we understood more about ADHD. I also wonder about implementing strategies class- wide to deal with situations.

On a final note, I know more about me and my ADHD then I ever did. I educate myself while I educate others. I create and manipulate coping strategies. I advocate and encourage accountability.

I motivate and inspire follow-through. It all helps. Especially knowing that others have ADHD; knowing that they experience many similar events; and recognizing that a family can be supportive and understanding. The educational system is designed to provide accommodations; we just need to recognize what accommodations they need. Then finally, acknowledging the value of services that are available for people diagnosed with ADHD – all of this combined can bring relief. I encourage everyone that has an interest in understanding others with ADHD to believe in them, help them and learn about ADHD. It starts with education, and strategies in order to manage, and be a success. My final thought is having an inner voice a mantra that can encourage accountability, success and maybe even follow-through. My mantra motivates me; the acronym **MESS,** has helped me to reach many of my personal and professional goals. It has guided me in a number of life transitions and of course in my professional role as an educator, an advocate, and a coach. I can only hope that awareness, education, strategies and perseverance will guide others on their journey to success. My intuitive character, my impulsive lifestyle and my ability to feel empathy, has been a journey; it leads to management, education, strategies and my success.

"I believe in myself; I believe in others with ADHD, and I accept my challenges. But most of all, I'm learning to embrace my strengths."

~Christina Johnson-Quan

REFERENCES

American Psychiatric Association. (2009) Diagnostic and Statistical Manual.

Barkley, R. (2007). *Attention deficit hyperactivity disorder in adults.* Jones and Bartlet Publishers.

Barkley,R.(2005).*Taking charge of ADHD.* New York, NY: The Guilford Press.

Carroll, A., Houghton, S. A review of the research on interventions for attention deficit hyperactivity disorder: What works best? *Review of Educational Research,* Spring 2002, 72(1) 61-99.

Curatolo,P., D'Agati, E.,&Moavero, R. (2010).The neurobiological basis of disorders(4th ed.) American Psychiatric Association.

Dupaul, G.J.,Weyandt, L.L., Janusis, G.M. (2011). ADHD in the classroom: effective intervention strategies. *Theory into practice*, 50, 35-42.

Harpin, V.A. (2005). The effect of ADHD on the life of an individual their family, and community from preschool to adult life. *Archives of Disabled Children.* 90: 2-7 6.

Lavoie, R.,(2007).The motivation breakthrough. New York, NY: Touchstone.

Learning Disabilities Association of Canada http://www.ldac-acta.ca/.

Learning Disabilities Association of Saskatchewan ADHD Coaching Manual 2011.

Levine, M. (2005). Ready or not, here life comes. New York: Simon & Schuster, Psychiatric Association.

Marchetta, D.J., P. M. Hurks, L. Hurks, J. Jolles. (2008). Interference control, working memory, concept shifting, and verbal fluency in adults with (ADHD). *Journal of Attentional Disorders. 53,65-75.*

Ramsay J. R (2002). A cognitive therapy approach for treating chronic procrastination and avoidance: behavioral activation interventions, *Journal of Group Psychotherapy Psychodrama and Sociometry.* 55.2-3,79.

Robin,A.L .(1998). ADHD in adolescence. New York, NY: The Guilford Press. Statistical manual of mental disorders(4th ed.)

Taylor, M., Hemingway, F., List-Kertz, M., Cordin, R. &Douglas, G., (2006). Responding to interpersonal and physically provoking situations: emotional intensity in children with attention deficit hyperactivity disorder. *International Journal of Disability, Development and Education.* 53:2, 209-227.

Whalen, C.K. and Henker, B. (1998). Attention deficit hyperactivity disorders. *Handbook of child psycholopathology.* (3rd ed.) Plenum Press. New York.

33571822R00081

Made in the USA
Charleston, SC
18 September 2014